Maria Takolander | The End of the World

New Poems

GIRAMONDO POETS

Maria Takolander | The End of the World

First published 2014
from the Writing & Society Research Centre
at the University of Western Sydney
by the Giramondo Publishing Company
PO Box 752 Artarmon NSW 1570 Australia
www.giramondopublishing.com

Designed by Harry Williamson
Typeset by Andrew Davies
in 9.5/16.5 pt Baskerville

Printed and bound by Ligare
Distributed in Australia by NewSouth Books

National Library of Australia
Cataloguing-in-Publication data:

Takolander, Maria –
The end of the world / Maria Takolander
ISBN 978-1-922146-51-9

A821.4

For my son, Samuel

Other books by Maria Takolander

The Double
Ghostly Subjects
Catching Butterflies
Narcissism

It's beautiful outside; like the end of the world.

I VITELLONI

Contents

1

2

3

1

Unborn

1. Morning Sickness

I had lost myself in a novel by Marie Darrieussecq
in which a woman grows bacon skin – broken by
hair that claws with its roots, coarser than on her
pudenda – and teats like gelatinous melanomas.
I saw her fretting and muddying the earth until her
rear end let forth a litter of mutant-lets, pink and
coarse as tongues and slippery. Their lids were serene,
as if eyes did not exist, and their ears were closed
to the sound of their own not screaming. It was then
I felt the tide come in, bearing silt stirred from the
fetid sea floor, old with starfish and eel bones. The
moon, for nine months, did not care to claim it again.

2. Ultrasound

I had read that some women feed life with scratched
hunks of earth that gravel their teeth, with the residue
of fire that sludges their gums, and with the odourless
powder their grandmothers used to stiffen petticoats
of crinoline. I imagine the starch creaming my throat grey,
and to us you look colourless as if you were made that way.
Still emerging from yourself, the bud of your nose alone
makes the universe less impossible. You do not know

that we are here, but this is how we watch you: on a
black-and-white plasma screen suspended on a wall
– the happy technician flicking us between dimensions
like Dr Who – and as if from an infinite distance.

3. Foetal Movement

In my guidebook to pregnancy, a pencil illustration offers me
a profile of myself: armless and headless, legs to mid-thigh,
only my reproductive organs and waste channels sketched in.
My abdomen encases an upside-down foetus above the
bulbous and textured outline of my rectal cavity, the muscular,
smudged passage of my vagina and my clear urinary tract.
The caption announces that by the end of the seventh month
the foetus can respond to taste, light and sound, and it can cry.
As I watch you shadow box with sourness, radiance and din,
the sources of which you must fear like a medieval Christian,
you make of my belly a theatre for unseen marionettes and
for pain that has no origin – except for the life I have given.

Post-partum

1

I lie in the dark like an amputated god,
leaking gangrene onto butcher's sheets,
clinging to the remote control for
the night nurse, bed, TV and lights.

Beyond the closed door there are labyrinths,
austere as heaven. I hear the midwives as
they promenade with their perspex bassinets,
our infants wrapped like bleeding limbs.

Through holes in their faces we call mouths,
the new flesh keens, quiets and keens, for a
dawn that none of us can see, but that I imagine
as crimson with rawness and never-ending.

2

They return you, wailing of the modern configuration
of a world that will not recede before your primitive stare,

but next to my body you hulk and settle. There you lie,
strangely hungerless, intense as a nucleus,

alive with an intelligence of I know not what.
Men wage war to make something this real,

but it was life, pure and gluttonous, that committed
this glorious violence upon you and me.

47 Degrees

After Black Saturday

Like succulents and the nocturnal,
my newborn and I keep secrets from the sun.

—

He consents to being lulled by the air conditioner
in the absence of my heart and lungs.

—

While we sleep, cots are x-rayed into molten,
and radiance seals the eyes of women and men.

—

Black-out. Torchlight in my child's room
catches his silent and swaddled watching.

—

The world, at dawn, is a tray for yesterday's cigarettes,
unattended for my infant and his lush bawling.

Night Feed

The TV before us is silent.

Planetary and darkling, you are
like the first-born human waking

to the light of a fire on his skin.

An evangelist weeps on a polished stage,
offering us his tour schedule:

Luanda, Rio de Janeiro, Rome,

faraway landscapes,
damaged like the moon.

Then a choir of women materialise

with red telephones,
their lips lustrous as enamel.

Greetings, they mouth, from modernity

to the time traveller at my breast,
who closes his eyes, drowsy again

from the pleasures of mammalian flesh.

The Arrivals

We saw it on TV, in black and white:
        the children were coming.

—

The days became dirty with time.
Dogs panted at the debris
        of a world already absenting itself;
        hollowing out.
An ordinary rock might kill a bird,
        though the sky was empty as a clothesline.
In the trees only the breeze swung:
        history passing.

—

Nights were a scullery,
        close as a womb.
It seemed like eternity.
We kept each other clean;
        pulled each other from dreams,
        like animals in all our shuddering and panicking.
Meanwhile the fire glowed;
        the knives on the table mirrored its flush.

—

It is true: we had kept the channels free
        in case they wanted to contact us.

Utopia

1

A caesarean section of the immaculate sky,
    And we were posed: twenty-something, marbled-limbed.
There were no membranous hollows in skulls
    Darkly sealing.
No teeth, dumb and insistent, beneath foetus-soft gums.
No guts racked by the victuals of mammals,
    The primeval composition of breathing.
No ova, milky and superstitious, buried within.
How the city shimmered;
    It shimmered with us.

2

We know the legends of the frightened ones.
How they founded intrigues on clumps of hair,
    Soil's hunger, ghosts thrown up by heaving seas,
    The chiasmic violence of trees.
How they pictured the universe, quaintly,
    As day or night.
By then words had emerged with the quality of mice,
    Soon desperate in their teeming.
Antibiotic, artistic,
    We were judicious in our purging.

Diurnal

The universe yawns,
cavernous as a mirror.

—

Half of earth's creatures:
star-struck and blind.

—

A dream, earth-bound
and sudden as a cockroach.

—

Night is true.
And not true.

—

Supple dawn light
blesses small spaces.

—

My son in his highchair
looks into a silver spoon.

The Interpretation of Dreams

For David McCooey

1

My dreams these days leave me to sleep.
In the unsound night my body is steadfast in its life support,

and in the morning I remember nothing
of the Machiavellian intrigues of my insomniac brain

as it reckons with paralysis and blindness,
a history of diurnal violence.

What lingers is only the sordid
and ordinary intuition that I am not what I seem.

2

Now here you are wrestling with the night,
your brain sparking your corpse like Dr Frankenstein,

as if life might grant you alone dark vigilance.
There is a field restless with scarecrows that send birds reeling,

which only your brain knows about.
Your larynx pushes out its cry for help

– the noise alien as a starling's.
I must wake you, quickly, so you do not disturb our son.

3

Within the undead body of our sleeping child
his brain is desperate as a Punch-and-Judy puppeteer.

There are fighting words: 'Mine! Mine!'
I write them down. But if I were a muse, rather than a scribe,

I would tender dreams that shimmer
like birch leaves and glow like moonstones,

not these darkling hallucinations of a brain
already wiling away the night on its pitiful past.

Sleep

And again you are fierce as a bear to night's imperative,
Its hiddenness.

There: the sounds of the animal.

How the dark years, those abominable millions of dark years,
Endure in this wombing.

The owl outside in the lightning tree:

Yellow-eyed as a ghoul.
When comes the slowing into plangency,

And the sun-quickened birds

Rally and remember to rail,
Believe none of it.

Your brightness, like theirs, is miniature.

Domestic

1. TV

The TV screen explodes
like an ice-cube camera-flash.

The house falls to the night,
the adults suddenly dead beneath

a threadbare purple coverlet.
They leave the dregs of the morning

to the children:
the glass on the carpet

so much grit and crumble.
The interior of the TV looks bereft:

a cardboard set grey-sprayed
with *Lost in Space* technology for effect.

Perhaps the two girls,
still in their pyjamas,

would have watched *Scooby Doo*.
Instead, they unsnib the glass door

and enter the hangover of summer.
On the tepid trampoline mat

in a backyard stacked with timber,
khaki-coloured tubes and dull steel,

they ignore the black-and-white collie,
old and obese, with dags

under its still-hopeful tail.
The dog stands in the dirt

under the shade of the eaves,
watching them.

2. Dressing Table

The wheels of the trolley are dark as ash
and uneasy on the shiny floor.

The girls in acrylic dressing gowns
watch their mother, contorted

under a fluorescent sheet,
disappear through a yawing gate,

their father urgent as the electric light
of the hospital corridor.

They wake to an empty house,
curtained, on a school day.

On a dressing table
there is a gold cylinder of lipstick,

a tube of mascara, and a compact
with three colours of eye-shadow –

green, blue-green and blue.
There are high heels

in the wardrobe
with the broken doors.

In sunlight enough to blanch the eyes,
they pass the line of spiked succulents

that seep milk when
their leaves are snapped.

A squat woman in a smock rushes
out from a screen door.

She catches them by their wrists;
draws them back into the shadows.

3. Pot Plant

In the backseat of a red Toyota
the girl rattles dull coins

onto a synthetic blanket,
yellow and cigarette-marked.

Her mother and sister watch.
The silver buys $10 of fuel

at the service station, luminous
as a city, and then they settle

for a dark place among eucalypts
further down the road.

When dawn breaks they enter
the hard light of the police station,

hardly dressed for it.
Two officers follow their car home.

There are fittings torn from ceilings,
books ripped from spines,

and a pot plant inside the TV,
terracotta shards, soil and roots littering

the room, as if Triffids had escaped.
And there is a man on a

velour-covered chair, his face broken
as the plaster walls around him.

At the refuge they find three beds
to a room, a formica table

around which women smoke,
and bars on every window.

2

Hotel Room

This is a place furnished by sanity.
The bed cover, beige, has been ironed of dreams.
TV channels, like zebras, are caged in a flat screen.
Food and drink are miniature, in hiding.
The toilet seat has been deftly secured.
Outside there are hallways designed by doctors.
A gentle choice: up or down.
The mirror on the back of the door seals us in.
As if 'do not disturb' means anything.

No Man's Land

There was no waiting: that was the thing.
We found ourselves – just like that – in the breach
    scarred by strangers and lovers, mothers and fathers,
    some charged by liquor, others discreetly civilized (until.)
How it all resembled the unearthly, even though
    there could be no mistaking all that wretched dirt.
Our bodies were real as the dying.
The wire, sheer metaphor, caught nothing: the ungainly fist;
    the blunt teeth; necks sinuous as horses'.
Corpses should have been raining from helicopters in the sky.
There were commands we knew – as we knew we lived
    secretly inside these bodies, which had these hands,
    this skin, these mouths – that were being broken.
At the end, alone, each of us felt raped by ghosts.
The mud was thick around our ankles.
Poppies would grow in the blasted space between us;
    yes, they would grow.

Crime Scene Investigation

The car deaf as a hearse
        from the screaming weight
of all that came before,
        we drive down a tarmac slashed
by white line, white line,
        into the splintered light
of the woods waiting,
        like eternity, just outside town.
We seek loam, incestuous
        with sodden bracken and leaf-rot,
homing to earth that gruels
        hair, skin, nails, flesh,
like its own,
        mulling bones for dogs.
There is no ground here
        for the posthumous,
its ceremonies and detectives.
        Psychology is impure as memory,
and anger a grubby friend,
        the loner we embrace
when we masturbate.
        Look: there is a birch leaf,
dazzling and uncertain,
        yet to fall
in this forest of late sun.

The Old World

Winter shrinks the world to a snow globe.
The barn keeps the cloven creatures
        out of death's litter.
Then the snow beds.
See the weighted boughs of the fir trees;
        the cloth-bound birch.
Whiteness has swallowed sound.
Look: there is a line of smoke, like a myth,
        escaping from the chimney of the bunkered house.

—

Summer's stream is somewhere, but you cannot see it,
        for the sticky grass;
        the trees delirious with mosquitoes.
The creek feeds a swamp without a name.
On a forest rock, marbled with slime,
        stands a lone elk,
        sudden as a storm.
See how the sun burns all night, like a promise
        of the end of the world.

Winter War

At dawn the birch trees are ice-smacked:
shocked and glassy.

The man limps across the snow,
his only illness memory.

Light presses against his eyes,
like a shard of the bottle

he broke over the night
– though it was the evening,

softer than skin, that had tempted him
from hiding.

He recalls the suckling: iron-bitter
as the earth, yet river-silken.

Then the black sky, pricked with stars,
like a medieval device,

and cold as iron.
How the birch trees,

pale as naked men,
were flayed against them.

Anaesthetic

For David McCooey

Valium-nice, this business of death,
this chemical smile

that floats my body, bundled in snow and hay,
above a hospital tray,

where flesh and time take wing like sin,
and I become

this white light and space,
pure, nothing.

Is this what they wanted,
those god-heavy trolls,

with their big hands and brown eyes,
as they crouched

with their mercury liquor under dank stone bridges,
year after year,

in thick grass or winter sludge, until they
drowned themselves there:

my great uncle, whose leg was shot off
among the mottled birch

where Soviet tanks ploughed the snow;
my youngest uncle,

who stole from his old mother to slake
his darkling thirst;

and my eldest cousin, who sunk into himself
to escape the inherited world?

Is this what I wanted in those leaden times,
when with every mouthful

I offered myself to the execution
of a putrid earth-bound history,

and is it what I am given now
only because I am godless and sober

(except when it comes to you)
and so careless as to be happy?

Meanwhile, Egyptian morticians manage
my corpse for resurrection.

I wake to the human condition
– mine anyway –

grateful to the miracles of science,
so much kinder than religion.

Thus returned to my body,
I await your certain coming.

Epilepsy

Years ago, from the dusk beneath the house
        (the earth there ash or sudden as bone),
my mother and I (on hands and knees, crook-necked)
        dragged our German Shepherd out into the soggy dawn.
The dog had only just died, but it was already like taxidermy,
        that final rigidity prefigured each time epilepsy struck
following those bleary-eyed and maddened bouts of roaming
        (as if the creature might escape what was to come).
My father would clap and call loudly (like a witch doctor),
        but there could be no distracting (dog or merciless man).

Days ago, with the Northern Hemisphere once again tilting towards
        the Sun (our planet silent about its grave mediations)
and the lakes beginning to unveil the mannequin trees
        (softening after the deep freeze), my uncle's corpse was found.
My mother, bereft of so many, once again called upon me
        to witness the crepuscular scene: the stranger
prone on the floorboards (face down) beside his unmade bed,
        the curtains still drawn, while outside mosquitoes blurred
the stagnant water and fields of redolent grass.
        There is hidden carrion: my uncle (shamefully meaningless).

If my mother had made me scuff and scrape under floorboards
        alongside her to fetch the stiff carcass of the dog,
perhaps it was because of all those times when (as a younger child)
        I skipped away from the telephone and its soundings of death

(away from a country resembling some cursed ice-bound kingdom).

This morning, I tell my son about his great uncle as we pass
the local cemetery in our fog-clinched car. He grows suddenly wistful
(like an old man) – 'so many of them', he says,
the maudlin knowledge an anomaly of his human brain, but fitful.
I point out, all gesture and cheer, a distant view of a sunlit hill.

Missing in Action

My great grandfather: lost to Stalin's purges
in a Karelian backwater of forests and sepulchral snow.
(The past is a deep but silent world.)

My grandfather: his heart stopped on the swampy farm in Mellilä,
where he dragged up life from the earth after the war.
(Hung over, he would beat the horses, their flanks shivering.)

My grandmother: dead soon after she got an electric stove,
her legs, from labour, covered in weeping sores.
(I heard her voice once, time-travelling through the telephone.)

My eldest uncle: dysentery got him as an infant in Karelia,
but life, seasonal, was not perturbed.
(Thirteen more, including my mother, inhabited the
same womb.)

My youngest uncle: alcohol.
He lived with his mother until the sodden end.
(He is round-faced, like a grown baby, in photographs.)

Three other uncles: heart attacks – possibly euphemistic.
(Pictures of those men, modest and blank-faced,
suggest something already buried.)

My cousin (and his wife): alcohol.
    Ilkka was tall and blurry around the edges;
    (I met him once, under an eternal sun, before he
    absented himself.)

My nephew: unfurling in a bicornuate uterus,
    far from that country infested by weather and history.
    (It was a pro-simian womb, so primitive that it ruptured.)

Mushrooms

Trailing after my elderly uncle and his grandson –
through the pagan tangle of forest and mosquitoes,
the sky glowering with an endless twilight,
the path clammy with grass – my uncle stops
and waits for me, just a tourist really. He points
out the *suo* – the bog – behind the murk of trees.
It is a sump layered with moss and looks solid.

Vaarallinen, he says – dangerous. My uncle
wears gumboots and carries a bucket for mushrooms.
The boy has a net for catching butterflies,
for sometimes spirits like that excite the air
before vanishing. My uncle, holding his grandson's hand,
is tall and erect, a champion at skiing and orienteering,
but nevertheless soft – *nassuja*, as they say – and often drunk.

There was midsummer's night, when he raised the flag
of the country defended by his father, who had killed so many
men resembling his brothers and sons. My mother always said
that my grandfather resurrected his enemies with a bottle,
loosing its sad genies into my grandmother's kitchen
during winter, when the iconic sun was in hiding
and the lakes in that land of mirrors sheeted with cold.

The flagpole on midsummer's night was planted (somehow)
on a granite rise, and my uncle could not stand by it for long.

This evening, though, he is sturdy and rational,
like the youth I imagined walking out of Karelia
with his parents and siblings when the Russians came,
their house burned down to the grave snow so that,
no matter what happened, their enemies would not find a home.

My uncle picks up manure – that of an elk – for me to inspect
and the glowing orb of a cloudberry, which disappears
into the silver-haired boy's mouth. Finally, he stoops beside
a growth of mushrooms, wart-like, sallow as the sky.
His grandson kneels too, exposing his pale neck.
The butterfly net is cast aside, and soon the mushrooms
are filling the bucket, with a soft but steady sound.

Huskies

Summer is luxuriating in its weight,
        and the sled-dogs, their eyes like ice,
flailing breath and spit, are fleeing

the mosquitoes, the moss-birthing granite,
        the riddle of trees, the lapping and seeping.
They had been chained under fir for days,

never barking, but howling their affliction.
        They hit the road, the dirt there tamped
and firm so that they gather speed like flight.

They hunt the future,
        the ethereal vision in the distance,
but they will never be fast enough.

Stalin Confesses

At my side I have concealed a child
        whose body was twice trodden by horses
hauling carriages through our boggy village,
        the hooves like machines.
The child's father, sludge-drunk and stone-fisted, beat him,
        as did his mother, full of God.
The seminary silenced his Georgian tongue,
        and the Russian army, even in war's thick, rejected him.
The child's face is smudged as the moon's.
        His memory, haunting his primitive skull,
is prodigious: he recalls the priest's stories
        and obscene glory, and every injury
cast upon his squat and pallid form,
        like Scheherazade for opportune recounting.
He hates fearlessly as only the fearful can.
        He damages others as only the damaged can.
His soul is a mirror of nature:
        a limpid marsh in a forest of the swarming.
Sometimes I mistake him for a devil;
        at other times an imp.
At home, he flicks cigarettes, drawn from his grubby lips;
        the embers land on my wife's skin
and do their slow work like smallpox.
        Not even he knows what he wants from her.
He leaves out my gun, weighty as a statuette,
        for my hopeless son,

who misfires it upon himself and, years later,
        throws his body like a bone bag
on the inflamed fence of a prison camp
        after the child continues to taunt him.
It is a death not without evidence
        of the kind that has proven satisfying.
At work the child lurks and watches:
        how the skin of the wretched changes colour
like a photograph in a chemical bath;
        how mouths move rabidly,
salivating like a dunce's or drunk's.
        Later I find him alone,
crouched like a deaf-mute, an illiterate,
        over the grave marks of typewriters,
the scratchings of pencil stubs.
        It is clear that he is looking for something.
He once entrusted to me a chronic dream
        in which his mother, father, unborn brothers,
soiled villagers in their carts,
        the priest in his finery, and even God Himself
will not, no matter the torment he inflicts on them,
        look upon his scorched soul
and confess they were responsible.
        In his waking hours he would believe such words
no more than the desperate who proffer them.
        He is certain only of death,
more biddable than life,
        and of how it makes all men sorry.

Chimney

By day it does its cumbersome work,
    only slowly,

clogged with the sweat
    of coal, meat, sticks and wood.

It is like a character from folklore
    – or something older – transmogrified

into this domestic hunkering
    of brick and soot.

—

In the evening it partakes of the ominous:
    the sky's transfiguration into night.

When the men and women have come and gone,
    like loaves of bread,

and the darkness solidifies and the children dream,
    the cold of the planets begins to seep in.

Before dawn, with the embers quiet,
    the chimney opens itself to the stars' alien light.

Convicts

Only a couple of hundred years ago, grown men and women
were child-small. Around England, everyone mattered less.
When people were hungry, they grabbed at bread made by bakers
with stubby fingers. When people died, planks were nailed together.
At all times, earth was easy to come by. After rain, bogs sucked
at the bald cart wheels of men and women trying to get somewhere.
In the cities, the cobblestones were grimy with children, drunks
and sluts. For money, some women hung out faded washing.
On the ocean, ships had low ceilings. For sailors, the toneless
creaking of wood and flapping of canvas sounded like direction.
Beneath the barrels of tack, the convicts listened to the magnitude
of the ocean and the wind, fixed to the clammy timber like snails.

White Australia

Black Caesar, a gargantuan escapee from a West Indian
sugar plantation, pilfered £12 from a dwelling house
in London – and was cast away with the First Fleet:
378 days on the purgatory sea to Botany Bay.

Sophie, a Malagay slave in Mauritius, torched a barn
housing a collection of leather straps – the flames soaring
like the sounds of the black horses inside – and was
packed off in a ship-sized crate to New South Wales.

Priscilla, in Jamaica, did not poison her master,
but she watched him purge his peculiar sickness
into his wife's bedpan – the ceramic one with floral motifs –
day after day, without great discontent.

A Khoi Khoi man, smaller than Ned Kelly and paler of face,
became a bushranger in Van Diemen's Land – although
Black Caesar, famous for his hard labour and gunmanship
among the Founders at Sydney Cove, was the first.

Before he bolted he even got a shot away at the Aborigine
Pemulwuy, who had killed the governor's gamekeeper;
(Pemulwuy took seven pieces of buckshot
that time and still did not go down in history).

Of course, the colonial office properly stopped it all,
but by then Martin and Randall, also among the Founders,
had set up Dixieland – outside Sydney – their progeny
spreading right across this wide brown land.

Eliza's Shipwreck

It was after the long boat was parbuckled
over the larboard gangway that the sea

revealed its measure to me, slapping the hull
all the stunned day and then the night,

more insipid and loathsome than any husband.
The men spat and stuffed the seams with strips

of leather and wrung their greasy hair,
but still the tepid water trickled in until

we were knee-deep like washerwomen.
I could say nothing of my three bairns

at Stromness, suddenly torn from my chest,
as if the heart of God no less had resided there,

nor of the one surrendered by my womb,
beneath my billowing skirts, silent as a fish.

When the sun and salt had seared my eyes,
I saw my children on an island strewn

with ice, frigid before a headstone,
their skin the colour of pigeon eggs

and their hats battened to their skulls
with the grip of something like my love.

Then the sea finally dispensed with us,
like a butcher casts his waste,

upon a plain of sand, vast and blowing
with despair. I saw those strangers

– their children – and I could no more stop
my keening than the desert dogs.

It was then I wrenched off my petticoats
and bid them tumble through the air,

my body emptied of prayer but delirious –
as a whore's, some will claim – for pardon.

Dogs in Space

Somewhere in Patagonia an old man carries an axe, and a kitten blows like tumbleweed down a street otherwise empty. The closed storefronts are vacant as dreams, and the traffic lights like absence before the raw wind. It is barely dawn.

At the bus stop, near a corner shop with flaking skin, the dogs begin to arrive, one by one, some greeting each other, silently, others standing or sitting alone. There is a dog with one eye, and another with three legs perched on the doorway ledge of the corner store, its windows boarded as if there was something terrible.

Then comes an old woman with a wooden cart, one wheel shrieking. When she stops she props the lid of her cart ajar for viewing. Soon the strangers come to look, their backpacks stuffed with sleep. Some arrive on foot, others in taxis. They bring the noise, and the day grows more sturdy.

The bus arrives like market day. And departs like evening. The dogs mill like litter in its lee. The old woman closes the lid of her wagon against the wind. The dogs cross the road, some alone, others together, to the lonely panic of the pedestrian lights.

The End of the World

Punta Arenas, Chile

It is Sunday afternoon, and the streets are ragged
as the wind hacking the polar Strait of Magellan,
the peeling paint of the docks, the stone banks,
the German street-clocks entombed by glass,
and the Plaza de Armas with its bronze statue
of the Portuguese captain who, half a millennia ago,
could not be found among the 18 sailors – once a pageanting 237 –
searched by the servants of King Carlos
when they drifted, stunned as infants, back into the waters
of a make-believe city in Spain.

Naked half-men had killed Magellan in the Philippines,
the Italian survivor Pigafetta said, before distracting
the heavy-jawed king, son of Juana the Mad, with tales
of the Patagonian giants he had seen at the end of the world,
– and it was true: the captain's eyes had blackened to the
ash-smeared warriors of Lapu-Lapu,
but they had filled with a night he had glimpsed
stowed in the creaking bowels of his ships,
in the relentless ocean, on the entangled shores (dreadful still
to Darwin,)
and within the frigid, star-circling sky.

Today the Plaza de Armas crawls with randy dogs
	while military personnel litter the park benches
like parasoled women, until the prettiest is dared to kiss
	the shine-worn toe of the bronzed Patagonian warrior
composed below Magellan and his cannon;
	suddenly unsmiling, he licks a bloody taste from his lips,
having condemned himself by lore to return to this place,
	where mongrels and Alsatians cling to any sex
in the eclipse of foreign trees and under the brittle sun,
	and where the cold will not let go of anyone.

Down the road in the museum (the invention of a madman
	who three times erected a cross, first of straw
and then of sticks, on a godforsaken promontory
	of the Tierra del Fuego, before wearing the devil-wind down
with reinforced concrete) century-old taxidermy exhibits death –
	pumas with moth-eaten ears and unhinged jaws,
condors black as gorillas, two Paraguayan heads like winter apples,
	and anaconda skin big as a man – while on a video loop
black-and-white Fuegians pretend to hunt and assemble huts,
	posing gap-toothed with family and ring-ins.

On the top floor there is a petroleum display – Enap, Methanex,
	Fasco – and a translated sign announcing,
With the time, the museum, very visited by residents and tourists,
	became extensive and notable,
along with plates naming the moustachioed founders of Punta Arenas,
	their skulls and cross-bones now encrypted

in the cemetery across the way, where angels dive among
        cypresses manicured into a wonderland silence
that takes the edge off death and the sight
        of all those abominable dogs, ranging everywhere.

Cusco

Old women sleep on footpaths next to cauldrons of boiling corn, the cobs with kernels as big and pale as teeth. They walk the hard roads with bundles of cans or sticks on their backs, like humps for lorries, oblivious to the ubiquitous mountains. Children in hand and lambs on frayed ropes, they offer themselves for photographs with their poppy-mouthed skirts and disease-reddened cheeks.

—

The street walls and foundation stones, born of an age of earthquakes and labyrinths, do not want for mortar or miracles. They have the science of the circling stars and the conquistadors' gods on side. In the church, Black Jesus, bathed in petals and candle smoke, grows smoother and darker each year, and the Blessed Virgin stands mountainous in a triangular dress, her spiked halo the Andean sun.

—

'Capitalism is misery and suffering,' laments the white paint on the wall of an adobe house, outside which a family with oxen and plough work the blood-soaked earth of the mountains that spewed up so much resilient and spectacular rock. They are watched by dogs, black and bald as pigs. Returning from the markets busloads of tourists, clad like cheer squads for Peru, take blurred photographs of the passing view.

—

The air congeals in our lungs. We are hungerless as the pure.
In the restaurant a woman vomits steak and chips into a side-dish.
Guinea pig is served here as at the last supper painted for the church
all those bloody centuries ago, when Judas wore a brown mask
and unrepentant stare. Back at our hotel room, the walls proven
against earthquakes, we are swallowed by silence as if by a tomb.

Buenos Aires

On a path, concrete as the shopfronts and sun,
a flame-haired woman has her neck licked
by a young man arch as Dracula.

—

The mothers smoking at cafés, collagen-lipped
and gravel-voiced, are fathers too for the men
with their ankle pants, snakeskin shoes and gum.

—

The gallery, white as Scandinavia,
casts its shadowless back on the relentless
railway tracks and chicken-wire slums.

—

Cats laze in the shade of an earth-quaked tomb,
stacked with coffins spilling skulls and bones,
generations of uncollected rubbish.

3

Cesare Lombroso, Criminal Anthropologist

After Criminal Man (1876) and The Female Offender (1893)

1. The Science of Criminals

Sample:
4 rapists, sparkly-eyed.
6 prostitutes, furnished thickly with hair.
3 thin-lipped murderers.
2 arsonists, both amenorrheic
 – at such an age when normal women are fertile.
7 thieves, all pregnant.
8 prepubescent masturbators.
5 forgers.
9 epileptic poets.
10 jug-eared drunkards, and
1 insane revolutionary.

Physiology:
Precocious development of the genitals
 – see my sketches of organs tattooed
 in prolix arabesques: 'You are a one-lira woman,'
 'It enters everywhere,' etc. –
High armpit temperatures.
Large jaw and receding forehead.
Webbed fingers and prehensile feet.

A bent nose, to the right or left.
Insensitivity to pain
– 'It is not true,' sang the gay swindler at the gallows,
'that death is the worst of all evils.'

2. The Criminal Case of Max Duke

Born 1720, hunter and fisherman,
wine drunkard and bushy seducer,
this semi-cretin became blind in old age,
his head heavy from a habit of eating mouldy polenta
– but not before producing the usual quantity of offspring.
Among his descendents I have found no less than
200 purse-snatchers, pederasts, deserters, and street urchins,
280 sick or impoverished individuals,
90 prostitutes or women with venereal diseases,
not a single one of the creatures bald.
These numbers do not include 300 childhood mortalities,
400 men infected with syphilis,
and 7 murder victims.
Such is the urgency of the situation:
by the time Max Juke died at the age of 75
he had already cost our state over 1 million dollars.

3. Criminal Behaviour: Of Origins and Cures

Tadpoles eat each other; crickets and pike too.
Science has witnessed organised theft among monkeys,
domestic burglary among cats, ants abducting minors,
and child abandonment among cuckoos.
Goats and bees are alcoholics. Tigers and hyenas
have bloodshot grey eyes identical to those of assassins.

Then there is civilization, celibacy,
a hot climate, and working as a shoemaker.
There are the months of June and July,
incitement to sex crimes;
May with its baleful influence on thieves;
and January, so provocative to forgers.

Few criminals come from the world of science,
while brigandage and poetry go hand in hand.
Thus literacy is no cure; I encourage
the learning of trades and gymnastics,
a priest's flare to the genitals, and incarceration
in isolation to halt the spread of infection.

I repeat: poetry is the language of the degenerate.
I offer an example, not unworthy of Petrarch,
penned by a Bedouin cook and poisoner:
'I am in the midst of evil Christians.
We are condemned to hell.
And you, mother, are outside crying.'

4. Coda: The Cesare Lombroso Museum

300 ragged-eyed skulls: Abyssinian, Chinese, Patagonian, Italian.
A mummy, drenched in coffee then wrung out to dry.
Models of carnivorous plants, human-sized.
A torn lithograph of a Prussian cannibal.
Pencil drawings by the criminally insane.
Scraps of tattooed skin.
Assorted bones – leftovers – from moonlit raids on Sardinian tombs.
The skeletons of murdered infants.
Miscellaneous weapons, manacles and leg irons.
A vast model of Philadelphia's Eastern State Penitentiary
  and its system of solitary confinement.
Death masks of a forger and murderer, resting on silk cushions.
The face of Cesare Lombroso, criminal anthropologist,
  soaked soft in an ancient jar of formaldehyde.
(His brain, according to the notes, is elsewhere.)

Degeneration

After Max Nordau's Degeneration (1892)

Let us expand the category of the degenerates
muddying this utopian age of pure
money and science, to include poets
(in addition to criminals, prostitutes, anarchists, and lunatics).

The problem with the poet is that she lacks the rigour
to adapt herself to the existing – the cause
of her dwindling – and becomes an idle meddler,
a cavalier visionary, monstrously ignorant of reality.

The danger of the poet, as with an ugly fetish,
is her power to exercise suggestion, although of course
those hysterics moved by her influence
are already, *ipso facto*, degenerate subjects.

Let it be said that poetry is atavistic.
It is a twaddle, a babbling and stammering,
that only imbeciles and academics profess to understand.
Clear speech, by contrast, is for capital minds.

(We must concede, however, that the poetical method
wielded by one such as V, notwithstanding
her asymmetric skull and pointed ears,
yields experiences that are perplexingly beautiful.)

Charcot's Patients

Meet the women of the Salpêtrière hospital in Paris:
    the homeless, the debauched, the epileptic, the old,
    those suffering from love, scrofula, cholera, nostalgia.
Once they were whipped on arrival.

Jean-Martin Charcot, the Napoleon of neuroses,
    prefers electricity, the ingestion of iron, suspension
    from the stone ceilings, and his own power;
he becomes known for his mesmerising salons.

He favours some patients over others:
    those with cherubic skin, ovaries
    available for compression, the flexible, the suggestible;
those who understand what he wants of them.

Having spied on Charcot's paintings (neo-classical),
    the women give him saucy tongues,
    open gowns, raised eyes, clubbed limbs,
religious ecstasy, arching, and such things.

Charcot offers interpretation, never forgetting appreciation.
    In the audience – among the artists,
    dark-coated doctors, and apprentices –
Freud knows instantly that he will abandon his study of eels.

Albert Londe, similarly inspired, develops a camera with nine lenses.
He clamps the women's heads,
then absconds behind a curtain thick as desire,
glorying them all with unctuous silver.

The women – many at the theatrical age of 16,
familiar with the attention of dour but excitable uncles –
pout and pray like the stars of early cinema.
Charcot's favourite quietly escapes, dressed as a man.

Years later – with Charcot posthumously celebrated
as the founder of Charcot's disease –
the Salpêtrière hospital in Paris receives
the body of Princess Diana, freshly deranged and photographed.

Golden Sigi: An Advertisement

I am actually not a man of science, not an observer, not an experimenter, not a thinker. I am by temperament nothing but a conquistador. – SIGMUND FREUD

The
legendary discovery by Sigmund Freud
(also known as Golden Sigi)
and
no other
of the magnificent narcissism of human beings.

Containing a sleepy account of the
memory of his mother,
rocking naked in the sluggish light
of the train
as she bent down to her bloomers,
her belly monstrous again.

The dreadful suffering of Golden Sigi
at the accomplishments
of his sister at the piano,
an outrage of wood and bones,
like a shipwreck
in their home.

The startling interpretation of his
illustrious destiny
in the witches of antique tragedy
and hermaphroditic eels,
all writhing, he perceived,
with envy.

The appalling treachery of
the anointed sons,
who swore on gold rings inset with
ancient intaglio
to give and forgive
him everything.

The final betrayal by Sigi's mouth,
indulged with cigars and
nestled within a soft beard
barbered daily,
which began to suffer ingloriously
from rot.

Show Business

The Parisian streets were rotten with sewage and offal. Butchers skinned and gutted beasts outside their shops. They passed off jawbones for cutlets; a man found teeth in his steak. Bread was scarce, and dried dog shit ground for pepper. Outside the perfumery, men on boxes barked of The Virile Boy and The Incombustible Spaniard.

Curtius' waxworks in those days had a Giant Negro for a doorman. Madame was the housemaid's daughter, a small and forgettable girl. She helped the master, whom she was permitted (delicately) to call Uncle, build a model of the impossible Salon of the Grand Couvert of Louis XVI.

As they positioned eyeballs, sewed hair into skulls – the young Madame had nimble fingers – dressed the horsehair torsos and timber limbs, and laid the table with papier-mâché poached eggs and chickens, Uncle talked. Some days, he said, the Queen's bouffant, studded with butterflies and cupids, would fit only beneath the heavens.

Fashions changed. Women in the streets wore short hair and guillotine earrings. Children paraded bearing cats' heads on stakes. Curtius, a businessman, came to arrangements: with Sanson, the executioner, for buttons; and with the trench-digger at the Madeleine cemetery. He took Madame there under firelight before the quick-liming.

They made moulds in the torch's half-night, sealing nostrils, coating eyes and swollen tongues, patting over the puckered rims of necks, with plaster that had always been – Madame saw it now – the colour of death. The tacky blood on Madame's apron, as her mother said, would never wash off.

Years later, Madame found herself married to a gambler. Napoleon would also soon prove bad for business. Working alone, she cast the face of her firstborn: a daughter, six months old. She watched as the corpse and the plaster hardened. She buried the child in a wooden box and kept the doll's mask. The show went on.

Witch

Her Hair was the Colour of Dirt, her Fingernails
of Stone, but she did not Lack Shelter or Know Hunger.
She Knew how the Body forces the Foetus to leave
its Mucous Womb and Breathe Air, and she could effect
Certain Remedies for Those Unwanted, rendering
the Creatures, While Still Hidden, Powerless. Small
Corpses were not Such a Problem. In the Summer Time
Birds and Foxes Picked them from the Fields, and in the
Winter Time they Nested in the Faggots on the Hearth Fire,
something her Mother, now Bedded by Soil, had shown her.
She had Seen, too, the Dark Heads of 11 Sisters and 1
Weird Brother being pushed through Blood and Faeces,
and had Learned to Avoid Men, Knowing What Happened.
Her Father, when Stopping, had only Ever Taken
of her Mother's Body, despite the 12 Sisters and the
Eerie Boy on the Beaten Ground. Her Visitors now
were Those Quiet Women, bearing Coins, or Sluts
if she was Needed to Call upon their Mistresses.
She had seen, on one Such Outing, a Churchman in a
Black Hat on the Muddy Road, Knowing what he was
and that He had seen Her, but she had Never Understood
his Arts: a Creature could not be Born without Sin;
and the Wine and Host turned into Piss and Shit, not
Blood and Bone, Man and Woman being Necessary

to make Those Things. But then came the Night when the Strange Men Took Her from her Warm Sack and Dragged her through the Grass to the Woods on the Other Side, near where her Mother Lay Buried. They Bound her Neck and Wrists and Ankles to a Tree Stacked with Kindling and Leaves and Forest Lumber and, as they Spoke Loudly of Heaven and Hell, the Male Essence and the Female Bowel, they Touched the Pile with their Flaming Torches, and she Found that she had Never Believed More in the Crucifixion.

Why Nuns Are Holy

Nuns are virgins.
    Their wombs, robbed of
    the worship of pagans,
    make us absent-minded,
    like corridors.

Nuns do not practice adornment.
    They do not beguile
    with ochre and emeralds,
    the omens that make
    bodies frightening.

Nuns are not garrulous.
    They take their language,
    surgeon-like,
    from a steel tray and
    are truly grateful.

Nuns are respectful.
    In stone convents, they
    hone themselves into ideas
    among the susurrations
    of long-dead men.

Nuns are holy.
So do not speak of it.
Or of how, month after month,
they bleed
like the unchristian.

Bestiary

1. The embalmed: beings from which life has been meticulously extracted like sap.

2. The stuffed: glassy-eyed beasts aghast at their own perversity.

3. The pickled: creatures, typically gangly, soaking in colourlessness.

4. Dinosaurs: works of funereal architecture.

5. Cannibals: opportunists, often mistaken for feather-and-bone ceremonialists.

6. The dying: organisms, to be eschewed, until such time as they heal from the open wound of living.

Loneliness

The donkey sat at the plastic table and looked at the sunset, the orange skyline quickening her like drunkenness or lust. She shook her head to shed the flies that clung to her weeping eyes and, before they settled again, saw the ibises in the swamp with heads like pick axes.

She turned to her husband. He was sitting beside her with a frayed rolled-up newspaper. He swatted his shoulders and legs, his tail twitching like an echo.

'Warm night,' she offered. She heard the sound of the flies around her ears and, more subtle, the stirring mosquitoes. The light was fading. 'Quite lovely,' she said.

Her husband smacked the green table. Three flies were dead.

There was something wrong with her, she thought. Some undiagnosed disease. It became insistent. Even as she knew she was being unreasonable, she turned on him. 'Do I even know you?' She regretted that her voice was so high-pitched.

Her husband sat, stooped, grey-haired, still. The sky was bruised, and the flies were dwindling. She found that she could not imagine, did not want to imagine, the underworld to which those insects were returning for the night. In the remaining light, the donkey looked at the sparse hair on her belly and watched as a mosquito landed, injected her with anaesthetic and filled up on her blood.

Violence

The goat fished from the old wooden jetty. A hangover, he thought, was a state of mind, like the stench of slimy pippies on the hook, the pull of dirty tide on the line. He wiped the residue of bait onto the tangled fur on his flank and picked up the thermos lid of coffee, the liquid cold as the dawn. The sea, he mused, always made him philosophical.

A couple of pelicans had settled on the peeling roof of the only boat moored among the mangroves, tucking their beaks into the rancid feathers of their backs. From time to time the goat saw their eyes, rimmed like a drunk's, move to watch him. It was no use; his bucket was empty. The fish, it seemed, had cleared out of this place. There were mud-crabs, exposed at low tide like rickety bones, and the usual detritus of birds. The landscape, though, had found a way into him. It was something his wife had never understood.

Sitting in the deck chair, the goat rested the rod between his pressed legs and poured some more coffee. He heard the sound of the slick water on the hull of the broken-down boat weighted by the pelicans. He swallowed some of the bitter brew and noted how the mangroves had spread. They were secretly closing the place in.

A seagull flew down from the anonymous sky and landed on the boat's stern. Its orange claws hooked the taffrail, and it began to vomit sound from its neck like something material. The goat pitched the fishing rod at the bird, and the pole landed, like a praying mantis, on the greasy water. The seagull stopped and looked at the goat. The goat saw that the bird had his measure.

Without blinking, the seagull took up the screeching again. The goat, hurling his chair and thermos into the sea, began to bleat and bleat in return.

The pig propped his hooves on the seat back and lifted the beer to his mouth. His toes, he saw over the translucent lip of the plastic cup, were perfectly clean if mottled in colour like the earth. The baying and howling intensified, and he turned his attention to the pitch.

The raccoon dealt with the first ball, tossed hard in the lull following the crowd's jeering. The ball rolled dead. A rat retrieved it, spat on the red skin and briskly rubbed it on the hairless skin of his groin. The next ball curved like the smell drifting from rot, and the racoon was out. Plastic cups flew up into the sky and down again like scuttled locusts. It had happened so quickly.

As the pig watched the racoon remove his helmet and return to the pavilion, he was momentarily unsettled. How fragile things seemed. How would they fill out the afternoon? The game, though, soon became robust and quite ordinary.

The pig might have dozed off, for time passed. When he woke there was a commotion beneath his grandstand. The pig looked down into the bay. An old emu lay on its back in a concrete aisle littered with plastic cups, cigarette butts, pie bags and miscellaneous stains. Two paramedics, grey wolves, knelt over him. One had its paws buried in the oily feathers on the emu's upturned and distended chest. The bird's legs hung from each side like snapped sticks. There was a small and sundry crowd.

Then from the other side of the arena, with a great wailing and roaring, came another wave of plastic cups, catching the sun, hovering and shimmering like angels. The partnership on the field had been broken. The pig found himself hurling his own empty cup into the teeming oval of the sky.

When he looked down at the aisle below, one of the wolves, its fur hoary as the grubby cement, had fetched a stretcher. Only the pig saw the wolves carry the large dead bird away.

The Gamble

The sky let loose – not a good omen – when the hare went to visit the polar bears. The bears greeted him, blocking the doorway, their fur bristling, black noses dry and porous like ice. They stank of dead fish and urine. They turned their colossal backs to him, and the hare followed them into the room, shaking his sturdy ears and skittering rain.

There was paisley carpet: brown with green eddies. The electric heater was on: a jittery orange glow. As usual there was a game going. At the table, draped with a crocheted cloth, was a horse, her back slumped with the ages, her eyes yellowed. Next to her was a moose with a scrap of fur missing from his snout. His antlers were intact. The drinking was being done from rank mugs. The ale was poured liberally.

The hare took a seat, picked with his teeth at a knotted mat of fur on his hind leg, and was dealt in. He sifted through the picture cards in his paws. Table talk was forbidden. In any case the hare was thoroughly preoccupied. He felt a familiar hunger for his own droppings – and something else, he only now began to realise, like a secret longing for his own death.

Flick-snap. He was struck by a jester wielding a cannibal's stick. The hare looked at the polar bear and at the stack on the doilied table. The bear's eyes were impossibly still and dark. The hare drank and wiped the froth from his mouth. He eyed the hunched paw of the bear as it turned the final card. Flick-snap. A black weapon shaped, it seemed to the hare, just like a scythe. He had lost everything.

The hare turned to the horse, who had closed her eyes. 'So, how about it?' he said to her, urgently, quietly. The mare opened her lashed lids and looked at him, he thought, with wist.

Just then the neighbourhood dogs came careening into the room, wet as the day, carrying on at the world as if something had to be done about it. The game, the hare knew, was over.

Acknowledgements

The poems in this collection have previously appeared in the following publications: the *Age, Antipodes, Australian Book Review, Australian Literary Review, Australian Poetry Journal, Axon: Creative Explorations, The Best Australian Poems 2009* (Black Inc.), *The Best Australian Poetry 2009* (UQP), *The Best Australian Poems 2010* (Black Inc.), *The Best Australian Poems 2011* (Black Inc.), *The Best Australian Poems 2012* (Black Inc.), *The Best Australian Poems 2013* (Black Inc.), *Blue Dog, Cordite, Eureka Street, Griffith Review, Heat, Hecate, Higher Arc, Island, Mascara, Meanjin, Michigan Quarterly Review, Moving Galleries, Notes for the Translators: By 142 New Zealand and Australian Poets* (Macao), *Overland, Southerly, Thirty Australian Poets* (UQP) and *Westerly.* My thanks to the editors of these anthologies and journals. Thanks are due to Kate Middleton, Fiona Wright and Lisa Gorton for supporting this publication. A special thanks to Ivor Indyk for making this a better book. My deepest thanks to my family and to David McCooey, whom I am blessed to have as a reader and husband.

This project has been assisted by the Commonwealth Government through the Australia Council, its arts funding and advisory body.

Australia Council for the Arts